Original title:
Island Winds and Tides

Copyright © 2025 Creative Arts Management OÜ
All rights reserved.

Author: Samuel Kensington
ISBN HARDBACK: 978-1-80581-646-1
ISBN PAPERBACK: 978-1-80581-173-2
ISBN EBOOK: 978-1-80581-646-1

Shadows of the Glistening Reef

The fish wear hats, quite a sight,
They dance and twirl with pure delight.
A crab with shades, so suave and cool,
He struts along, the ocean's fool.

The coral sings a silly tune,
While turtles spin beneath the moon.
A lobster jokes, it's quite a show,
He tells bad puns, but we all go slow.

A Voyage Through Celestial Currents

A sailor's hat, but where's the boat?
With fish that claim they've learned to float.
The sky, it giggles, clouds like sheep,
They pop and bounce, not one to keep.

The stars are squabbling, what a fuss,
One says, 'Shimmer!' the other, 'Blush!'
A comet zooms, with style and flair,
Just passing through without a care.

Breath of the Surging Waters

The waves come in with goofy grins,
They tickle toes and pull at fins.
A seagull squawks, "Who stole my fries?"
It flaps away beneath the skies.

The clams are laughing, what a riot,
They're boasting tales of their own diet.
A starfish waves, "I'm quite the star!"
While sea cucumbers whisper, "Not by far."

Embrace of the Twilight Breezes

The breeze tickles with a gentle tease,
It swirls around, like playful bees.
A squirrel capers, stealing snacks,
While shadows dance, avoiding "tags."

The laughter swells, it fills the air,
As crickets chirp with joyful flair.
The moon rolls in with a wink and grin,
Saying, "Let the fun – begin, begin!"

Whorls in the Moonlight

Stars giggle as they shine,
The sea calls out, 'Come dine!'
Fish in ties do tango swirl,
Jumping high, they make us whirl.

Lobsters wear their crabs' old shoes,
Snails with flair throw wild views.
Seagulls squawk a funny tune,
Moonlit waltz beneath the dune.

Where the Horizon Meets the Dream

Kites fly high, tangled with bliss,
The ocean waves give a cheeky kiss.
Sandcastles rise with sandy flair,
But watch out, the tide has a dare!

Mermaids laugh with jellyfish,
Creating a splashing, silly dish.
Octopuses juggle shells with glee,
Underwater circus, come and see!

Nature's Invitation to Wander

Breezes whisper secrets bold,
Stories of sun and sea retold.
Crabs on stilts prance with pride,
While turtles take a funny ride.

Footprints lead to a giggle race,
As gulls join in, a funny chase.
Nature's brush paints smiles on trees,
Laughter echoing on the breeze.

Winds of Change on the Open Sea

Sails flap like flags in a dance,
Waves tumble, giving fish a chance.
Squid in bow ties sing off-key,
Dance party hosted by the sea!

A parrot jokes with a wise old whale,
Together they spin a wobbly tale.
As dolphins giggle, they plot a spree,
Comedic chaos, under the sea!

The Chorus of Soft Raindrops

Pitter-patter on my hat,
Dancing droplets, imagine that!
They tap my nose, they swirl around,
A silly band that won't be drowned.

Splashing puddles, big and bright,
Jumping high with pure delight!
They giggle as they race and roll,
A playful tune to grace the soul.

The Gentle Pull of Distant Shores

Oh, those shores call out to me,
With whispers sweet like lemonade tea.
They tickle my toes, then retreat fast,
A cheeky game, a one-day blast.

I chase the waves with much delight,
They sneak away, just out of sight.
But they laugh back, a bubbly cheer,
For every splash brings joy, I hear.

Beneath the Glistening Veil

Underneath the glittering haze,
Curious crabs join in the craze.
They throw their shells with much finesse,
Dancing 'round in a sandy dress.

The fish flick tails like playful darts,
They splash and swirl, oh what fine arts!
Beneath the shimmers, tricks unfold,
A show of laughter, bright and bold.

The Odyssey of the Sail

A sailboat bobbing, what a sight,
With cats chasing seagulls in flight.
The captain sneezes, "Ah-choo!" he shouts,
And suddenly, the wind's in droughts.

But with a wink and a twist of fate,
The sail catches wind, oh, isn't it great?
They zoom and whirl across the foam,
That boat is now a rolling home.

Salty Kisses on Weathered Skin

Sunburned noses, laughter loud,
Crabs dance sideways, oh so proud.
A kite takes flight, then takes a dive,
Chasing seagulls, feeling alive.

Flip-flops squeak, a slippery race,
Sand in shorts, oh what a place!
Mermaids giggle, not quite real,
As we sunbathe, they steal the wheel.

The Melody of the Rising Tide

Shells sing softly, waves applaud,
Watermelons roll, what a fraud!
Fish wearing hats swim by in glee,
Join the parade, come dance with me.

Seashells whisper, secrets to tell,
Where did my sandwich go? Oh well!
The ocean's laugh, a bubbling tease,
Washing up socks, oh what a breeze!

Soft Footprints on Weathered Dunes

Sandcastles crumble, oh the fate,
A seagull snatches lunch—what a trait!
Sandy toes wiggle, trying to hide,
As crabs march forward, full of pride.

The sun sets low, a disco ball,
Shadows dancing, we have a ball.
With beach balls flying over my head,
Playing dodgeball with seaweed instead.

Forgotten Echoes by the Shoreline

Whispers of laughter float through the air,
A beach ball sails without any care.
Forgotten treasures lie in the sand,
A sock, a flip-flop—oh isn't it grand?

Turtles in shades, slow-moving race,
Flip-flops strapped tight at a hilarious pace.
Echoes of giggles, a chorus of cheer,
The tide will take all, but we won't disappear!

The Solitude of Sandy Retreats

In a hut made of seaweed and dreams,
The crabs throw a party, or so it seems.
They dance on the sand, a comical crew,
While I sip my drink, shade provided by a shoe.

Seagulls dive-bomb like they're on a quest,
For a fried feast, oh what a jest!
I dodge and I weave, sipping my brew,
Unknowingly joining this aerial zoo.

The waves crash in with a frothy laugh,
Salty sea foam, nature's own gaffe.
As I build my castle, it parts with a giggle,
The tide claims my fortress, oh how I wiggle!

Even the sun joins this whimsy parade,
Playing peek-a-boo, giving me shade.
With laughter so loud, I can barely compete,
Nature's own joke, so absurd and sweet.

Where Water Meets the Sky

The horizon winks, it's a cheeky affair,
Clouds wearing sunglasses as if they don't care.
The ocean splashes back, in vibrant replies,
Waves rolling in, as if to surprise.

Fish flip and flop, throwing a show,
With fins as their flares, they put on a glow.
A dolphin breaks through, with a snicker and spin,
Challenging seagulls, 'You start, I'll win!'

Sunset paints colors, a carnival prize,
While I munch on snacks, with chips on my thighs.
The gulls start a choir, out of key they sing,
But the surf joins in, what joy they bring!

An octopus juggles, oh what a sight,
He drops all his balls, it's sheer delight.
As laughter and waves mix, I clap and I cheer,
The stage of the sea, where mirth is near.

Shifting Silhouettes Against the Sun

Shadows flicker and dance with delight,
As palm trees twist, bidding farewell to night.
A crab in a tux, with a monocle tight,
Claims he's the chef of this beach restaurant right!

Footprints in the sand tell stories quite bold,
About a sandcastle, once glorious and gold.
It vanished with laughter, a tide-twisted fate,
"Who needs bricks?" I shout, "Let's elevate!"

Kites soar above, like comedy troops,
Tangled in laughter, the whole world loops.
While wanderers jog, with shoes all askew,
Each misstep a giggle, chasing the view.

And as the sun sinks, the colors explode,
A painter's palette, on nature's abode.
The silhouettes mingle, a comical scene,
Where every wild laugh feels like a dream.

Arbor's Secret Beneath the Waves

Beneath leafy whispers, secrets unfold,
Mermaids gossip, they're terribly bold.
With shells as their phones, they share juicy tales,
Of fish-fry feasts and their grand ocean sails.

The tide tugs at roots, in a mischievous way,
Where seaweed sneaks in for a leafy buffet.
A crab holds a party, all shells on parade,
While I sit and ponder how jellyfish wade.

Coral reefs giggle, they dress up in hues,
While the clownfish tease, in their colorful shoes.
Anemones bounce, like they know a secret,
But their jokes are so cheesy, can't help but regret!

So next time you ponder, beneath the large trees,
Know that the ocean's got stories to tease.
From fish in tuxedos to secrets so bright,
This underwater circus brings pure delight!

Whispers of the Ocean's Breath

A crab in a tux, takes a stroll,
Pokes fun at the fish, but forgets his pole.
The waves giggle softly, a ticklish glee,
As barnacles dance, sipping tea by the sea.

Seagulls hold court, on a rocky throne,
Disputing the price of a clam's old bone.
They caw with such flair, debating their fate,
While sandcastles crumble; oh, such a great date!

Jellyfish float by, with style so bright,
Waving their tentacles, a comical sight.
They laugh at the dolphin, all flips and all spins,
As the ocean shares secrets with mischievous fins.

The tide rolls in, with a mischievous grin,
Telling the shoreline it's time to begin.
A game of hide-and-seek, with the lost flip-flop,
As crabs do a dance, and the chuckles won't stop.

Secrets in the Sea's Embrace

A clam in a shell, whispers so low,
Telling tales of a fish, with a bright yellow glow.
The octopus giggles, with secrets to keep,
While starfish are lounging, in slumber so deep.

A sea turtle races, but don't be misled,
For a jellybean jellyfish just pulled on his thread.
They shared a quick laugh, at their silly old race,
While seaweeds sway gently, in a graceful embrace.

The pufferfish pouts, in a ticklish debate,
Inflating his ego; oh, isn't he great?
Seashells chuckle softly, in an echo so sweet,
As the seafoam does tango, with bubbles at their feet.

Waves crash in rhythm, a dance to behold,
Tickling the toes of the mermaids so bold.
They sing out of tune, harmonies on tide,
While crabs tap reminders: "It's fun to collide!"

Moonlit Currents and Starlit Shores

At night, when the sea is a shimmering spree,
A frog on a log croaks, 'Come dance here with me!'
The moon winks down, with a silvery smile,
As fish pull off pranks, it's their favorite style.

A dolphin leaps high, tail flicks with a cheer,
Challenging a clam, in a friendly veneer.
The starfish all giggle, and join in the fun,
As crabs break the rules, they can't be outdone.

The nights are a riot, with creatures galore,
Glow-in-the-dark jelly, gliding ashore.
With laughter and spritz, the cool breezes send,
As the sea comes alive, on the ocean's soft bend.

Stars twinkle above, saying 'Oh try a new game!'
As the ocean's offspring, all join in the fame.
With surfboards of foam and a whimsical glide,
Every creature's a star, with no one to chide.

Echoes Beneath the Blue Canopy

Bubbles burst forth, with a giggle and pop,
As fish-teasing laughter rings out from the top.
A sea cucumber rolls, with an effortless flair,
While underwater echoes tickle the air.

The squids play charades, in a dramatic display,
With ink-splattered plots that lead hearts astray.
They twist and they turn, in a glittery whirl,
While a shy little snail gives a wave and a twirl.

Seashells exchange secrets and glittery vibes,
As clowns of the deep pull off marvelous jibes.
They jest about treasures, and hoards made of sand,
While dolphins do flips, forming conga lines grand.

Anemones sway, silly songs they compose,
As the tide brings a wink from the sea's little prose.
Every creature enacts, a whimsical cheer,
In this watery world, where laughter draws near.

Beneath a Canopy of Stars

Underneath the twinkling lights,
A crab attempts to dance with might.
The seagulls squawk, they steal the show,
As waves keep laughing, 'Oh, hello!'

A starfish thinks it's quite a star,
While swimming shells all shout, "Folk art!"
The moon looks down, it winks at me,
As fish throw parties, wild and free.

Currents that Call to the Heart

The tide proposes, 'Come on out!'
With seaweed hugs and whispery shout.
A jellyfish floats, soft and bright,
Saying, 'Dance with me all through the night!'

The gulls can't keep their beaks to themselves,
They're squabbling over beachy shelves.
A clam drops pearls like it's confetti,
While dancing with a crab named Betty.

The Swell of Time and Memory

Time rolls in like a big old wave,
With memories tucked, it's hard to save.
Seashells giggle on the shore,
While little kids ask, 'Is there more?'

The tide ticks by, a playful tease,
As sandcastles melt easily with ease.
A porpoise jumps, it's quite the sight,
Saying, 'Let's party! We'll be here all night!'

Vows Written in the Sand

Lovebirds scrawl names in the soft white sand,
While goofy crabs hold a wedding planned.
The magic of waves will wash it away,
But they don't care, they'll just stay and play.

A flounder frowns, 'You missed the spot!'
And a mermaid sighs, 'Well, isn't that hot?'
As laughter dances on the salty breeze,
With vows declared beneath coconut trees.

Tales Carried by Oceanic Whispers.

A crab named Fred wore a hat,
He danced on the shore, how about that?
Seagulls laughed as they flew by,
Fred tipped his hat and gave a high five.

A clam once tried to play the drums,
But lost his groove, oh how it hums!
The shells all rolled, they couldn't keep tune,
While fish swam by, chuckling at noon.

A starfish dreamed of being a star,
But struggled hard with the guitar.
He tried to jam with a jellyfish band,
But only made jello, much to their planned.

The tide pulled in with a mischievous grin,
It tickled the beach and invited a swim.
"Come have some fun!" the waves seemed to call,
While the sand yelled back, "This party's for all!"

Whispers of the Coastal Breeze

The breeze tickles cheeks with a laugh,
As crabs hold a race, what a daft!
A pelican swoops, looking for lunch,
But finds a potato, oh what a bunch!

Seashells gossip, "Did you hear,
That fish took a selfie, oh dear!"
They giggle together, all in a row,
While barnacles wax poetic, just so.

A dolphin's flip causes quite the splash,
But tripped over seaweed, oh what a crash!
"Are you still there?" calls the tide with glee,
"Come join the circus, just wait and see!"

The sun sets low in a colorful show,
As the waves sigh softly "What a day, whoa!"
The laughter continues, the night's so divine,
Under the moon's watchful, silvery shine.

Echoes of the Sea's Embrace

A seahorse wore a bowtie with flair,
He twirled and spun, like he just didn't care.
The octopus clapped, eight arms in the air,
"Join the parade!" came the call from the fare.

The fish held a birthday with kelp for a cake,
But the crabs stole the frosting, oh what a mistake!
Bubble-blowers laughed at the scene quite absurd,
While the stingrays reported it all, with the word.

A sea cucumber slid down for a dive,
Tumbled and giggled, feeling so alive.
The waves rolled in, cheering "Hooray!",
As the ocean floor hosted its wild cabaret.

However, the tide reminded with a wink,
"Don't take too long, or you'll sink!"
With laughter echoing, they all took their place,
Leaving behind bubbles in a joyful chase!

The Dance of Ocean Currents

The currents swirled with a chuckle and jig,
While barnacles boogied, oh what a big gig!
A flounder slipped through the dance floor's tide,
As clams cheered him on, all filled with pride.

Seaweed's the star, oh what a wiggle,
Ballet of bubbles, the shells all giggle.
A nautilus twirled, shouting, "What's the fuss?"
While nudibranchs said, "Dance with us!"

Whales serenade with a humorous tune,
Echoing laughter beneath the moon.
They flipped and splashed, causing quite the stir,
As the dolphins chimed in, "We need to concur!"

The tides broke out in a giggly spree,
Inviting all creatures for fun at sea.
With waves as their partners, laughter was free,
What a grand gala in aquatic jubilee!

Dance of the Salty Zephyr

A gusty guest at my seaside door,
Turns my hat into a soaring soar.
Chasing crabs that scuttle and flee,
Laughing at a kite stuck in a tree.

Seagulls squawking their funny songs,
While flip-flops dance where the wave belongs.
My sandwich flies, a swift little thief,
I guess it's lunch in a world of belief.

The shore's shell dance in a jolly cheer,
Bouncing away in a pirouette near.
Feet in the sand, a tickling spree,
Oh, the wind knows how to tease me!

Sunset laughter, the tide returns,
Dancing with shadows, the magic churns.
The salty breeze whispers with ease,
"Life's a beach, so let's giggle, please!"

The Call of Distant Horizons

A boat with dreams sails on a whim,
While my snack flies off, no chance to swim.
A fish throws parties with deep-sea glee,
I join in, pretending to be free.

Laughing waves, they tickle my toes,
Making footprints that the tide bestows.
As gulls gossip about yesterday's news,
I wonder if they know how to cruise.

The starfish threw on a fancy hat,
While crabs insist they can do a spat.
Distant shores whisper of bright new finds,
With every laugh, I chase the winds' binds.

Under the sun, with a grin so wide,
I shake my fists at the playful tide.
Each wave a joke, a dance in the foam,
In salty realms, I find my home.

Driftwood Dreams on Gentle Waves

Driftwood lies like a sleepy friend,
With tales to tell that never end.
Tide pools giggle with tiny shrimps,
While I ponder why I have such wimps.

A rubber duck floats valiantly by,
Chasing a crab with an unblinking eye.
My flip-flops flee, they've got their own game,
Running from seaweed, what a shame!

Seashells whisper secrets of cheer,
While jellyfish do silly ballet near.
The salty air fills with stories spun,
About a crab who dreamed he could run.

Sunset paints the horizon so bright,
I start to dance, it just feels right.
With driftwood dreams and laughter in tow,
I wade into the fun, forget the woe.

Serenade of the Coral Sands

The coral sands hum a tune so sweet,
While clam shells gossip beneath my feet.
A sea cucumber struts with delight,
Making friends with a fish in the night.

Starfish adorned with a sparkly crown,
Confidently walk all over town.
I join the parade, just follow the beat,
With a conch shell blowing, we can't be beat!

Waves clap their hands as they splash and play,
While sandcastles threaten the tide's sway.
A crab in a tuxedo takes center stage,
With a wink and a jig, he engages!

Under the stars, with laughter so bright,
The evening flows in pure delight.
From coral sands to depths unknown,
In this watery tale, I feel at home.

Refrains of the Ocean's Song

Seagulls squawk like they own the place,
As starfish dance in a slow embrace.
A crab in a tux, adjusting his tie,
Waves splash laughter beneath the sky.

Beachballs bounce on a windy spree,
While sunburned tourists sip iced tea.
A dolphin pokes fun at a clumsy flipper,
Winking at fish with a cheeky quipper.

Sandcastles tumble like jokes gone wrong,
As kids all sing an off-key song.
The rhythm of surf, a quirky beat,
Feet in the sand, oh isn't it sweet!

Caught in a net of silly delight,
Jellyfish wiggle in the moonlight.
The ocean's giggle is hard to resist,
With each wave crashing, a merry twist!

Beneath the Moonlit Canopy

Crabs in the moonlight stumble and sway,
Practicing moves for the dance of the day.
The shadows stretch like they're having fun,
While fireflies buzz, their work never done.

A starfish rolls over, feeling quite sly,
Says to the seaweed, 'Oh me, oh my!'
Fish swap their gills for Brazilian flair,
As dolphins descend for a moonlit dare.

Whales join the chorus, crooning a tune,
While octopuses juggle in the light of the moon.
The tides pull back, giggling with glee,
As laughter echoes where the sea meets the spree.

Shells hold secrets of laughter and cheer,
Whispering tales that all creatures hear.
With a flip of a fin, they all start to tease,
Nature's own party beneath the tall trees!

Lullabies of the Forgotten Coast

Sand dollars whisper sweet bedtime rhymes,
As crabs play maracas, keeping the time.
The breeze hums softly, a song full of cheer,
While seahorses sway without any fear.

Old boats creak tales, with a comic twist,
Of mermaids who frolicked and swam in a mist.
Driftwood giggles, telling stories of old,
Of fishy adventures, both daring and bold.

The sun winks in, painting skies bright,
As starfish confetti dances in light.
Beneath tattered sails, humor's on deck,
Where sea creatures laugh at the captain's old speck.

With tickling tides and bubbles so free,
The shores sing softly, a magical spree.
Once forgotten, now filled with delight,
With lullabies echoing into the night!

Traces of Time in Every Grain

Time slips away like a crab on the run,
Burrowing down, saying, 'I'm just having fun!'
Seashells giggle, with whispers so sly,
In each little grain, a story awry.

Old fishermen weave tales of their catch,
While the gulls below just belly laugh and scratch.
The ocean's a clock that ticks in reverse,
Counting laughs rather than any old verse.

Ripples race past like children at play,
The tides keep us guessing, night turns to day.
With ocean spray painting smiles on our face,
Each grain holds a secret, a funny embrace.

So here we stand on this whimsical shore,
With tales in our hearts that we simply adore.
In each little footprint, a memory etched,
That time laughed a little, and love simply stretched!

The Voyage of Soaring Pelicans

Pelicans glide with a clumsy dance,
Snatching fish in a comical trance.
They bump, they flop, oh what a sight,
Chasing dinner in joyous flight.

Splashing down like feathered fools,
Their fishing skills break all the rules.
With beaks wide open, they dive and plunge,
Who knew they'd get so wet in their grunge?

They cackle loud and flap their wings,
Making a racket, oh, the joy it brings!
A wriggly fish becomes their prize,
But straight from the catch, it leaps—what a surprise!

And as the sun sets, with fishy glee,
These goofy birds are wild and free.
In their chaotic, playful spree,
Who needs a boat? Just enjoy the spree!

Murmurs of Salt and Seaweed

In the briny mix, the seaweed sways,
Whispering secrets through its gooey maze.
A crab scuttles by in a hasty escape,
While seaweed giggles—what a funny shape!

The seagulls squawk a raucous tune,
Dancing on waves beneath the moon.
A catchy tune from the ocean's lip,
As fishy jokes make the currents flip.

Tangled limbs of kelp, a slapstick scene,
Creating chaos, but who knows what it means?
With every wave, a bubbly laugh,
In the brine of life, we sail our craft.

Among the fishes, still and sleek,
A seaweed band plays hide-and-seek.
With salty pranks and merry play,
Laughter echoes, come join the fray!

Sails Against the Horizon

With sails unfurled, we aim to glide,
Across the sea, what a silly ride!
The wind's a wild, unkempt beast,
Sending us tumbling, yet we feast!

The captain shouts, "Hold on tight!"
As the boat rocks left and right.
A sudden wave, a slosh of brew,
"Is this adventure or water zoo?"

Fish poke their heads, giving a cheer,
As our boat bounces, no room for fear.
We laugh and sputter, drenched in spray,
With each wild wave, we dance and sway!

So here we sail, with snacks in hand,
The open ocean, our goofy land.
We hoot and holler, what a delight,
Embracing the sea with all our might!

Kaleidoscope of Ocean Colors

Colors swirl in the bubble parade,
Fishes flash like they're mislaid.
A rainbow reef and playful hues,
Make every dive feel like a cruise.

Corals poke out, all wild and bold,
Telling jokes that never get old.
An octopus twirls with flair and fun,
Spinning tales under the sun.

A dolphin slips and slides with glee,
In this whirlpool of color and sea.
With flip and splash, it steals the scene,
Making every day feel like a dream.

As the sunset melts into the tide,
We wave our arms and take the ride.
In this bright world, we laugh and play,
With colors shining in ballet!

When the Foam Speaks

The bubbles giggle with delight,
As they tumble and splash in flight.
"Hey there, look at me!" they tease,
Dancing on waves with the greatest ease.

Crabs join in, they tap their claws,
Skipping beat with snipping jaws.
A fish pops up, all dressed in flair,
"Wish you could see my water hair!"

When the seafoam starts to sing,
Jellyfish twirl in a goofy swing.
Seagulls laugh, they join the show,
"Don't you dare get too close, or you'll glow!"

But as the sun dips low from view,
The foamy fun bids us adieu.
With saline smiles and salty cheer,
The ocean whispers, "Same time next year?"

Reflections in the Water's Eye

A mirror floats, it's quite a treat,
Often splashed by a skipping feet.
But when a wave rolls in with style,
It swirls my face and makes me smile.

I see a fish make funny faces,
As it zooms past in silly races.
"Copy me, I'm slick and new!"
Said the flounder, with one shoe askew.

The clouds drift by and start to skate,
Playing tricks, it's never too late.
A duck in sunglasses glides with ease,
"Life's a splash, come ride the breeze!"

But as night falls, the tricks grow bold,
Fish whisper secrets and tales retold.
In the water's eye, the pigments gleam,
"Watch out for the next wave, it's a wild dream!"

Grauers and Glimmers of the Deep

Down below, the party's lit,
Where grumpy crabs have quite a wit.
"Who's wearing which shell tonight?"
"Mine's the shiniest, it's pure delight!"

An octopus juggles clams with flair,
As the sea cucumbers sway and stare.
"You think your shells are nice and neat?
I've got a talent for funky beats!"

The fish parade, they're proud and bright,
In colors that sparkle in the night.
Turtles roll by, cracking jokes,
"Just don't ask about our old folks!"

But when the current starts to sway,
All creatures know it's time to play.
With grinners and glimmers, the ocean's fun,
"Join the dance before we're done!"

Dance of the Shimmering Surface

The waves break out in a jig and leap,
While sunbeams bounce, it's never cheap.
"Who can do the highest backflip?"
Chortling dolphins take a dip.

The shadows of fish, they swirl and glide,
In a polka beneath the tide.
"Watch your back, here comes my spin!"
They whirl around, with a grinning fin.

A starfish yells, "I'm ready now!"
"Let's take a bow, we'll wow the crowd!"
With seaweed wigs, they sway in time,
Creating waves of silly rhyme.

As the sun dips low and day feels grand,
The shimmering crew takes a hand in hand.
"We'll dance again at the next sunlight,"
The waves whisper soft, "With all our might!"

Journeys Beyond the Known

I set sail with a sandwich in hand,
The sea's my ride, ain't life just grand?
A fish waved hello, it splashed with glee,
I shouted back, 'Hey, come sail with me!'

The boat did a jig in the salty spray,
My hat flew off, oh what a ballet!
A dolphin flipped, I clapped with delight,
Then promptly fell in—it gave me a fright!

The map's upside down, oh what a sight,
I'm heading south when I meant to go right!
The compass is spinning, my ship's in a spin,
Maybe it's time to just let the fun begin!

As waves danced around, I laughed at my plan,
The seagulls were roasting a sardine can.
I joined in the feast, what a wild midday,
In this crazy journey, I'll eat my way away!

The Call of the Gull's Flight

A gull landed on my sandwich stack,
'Excuse me, mate, you've got a knack!'
I laughed and tossed it, a morsel of bread,
He flew off grinning, my lunch now shed.

The wind played tricks, it twisted my hair,
I felt like a scarecrow without a care!
A crab waved hello, with a sideways dance,
With all these antics, I couldn't help but prance.

The laughter echoed from waves to shore,
As I partnered with nature, who could ask for more?
With every breeze, my worries took flight,
In this silly world, everything feels right!

So I'll cherish the chaos, the fun in the mess,
For life's little whims, we must love and bless.
A gull by my side, a friend on the roam,
With him, I found my sea-foam home!

Horizon's Edge and Shadows

At the horizon's edge, I squinted my eyes,
Saw a ship made of candy, what a surprise!
With jellybean sails and a lollipop mast,
I hopped on board, wondering how long it'd last.

The captain was a parrot, quite full of sass,
He squawked out orders as we sailed past glass.
With crew made of kittens, we laughed at the waves,
Making memories full of giggles and braves.

We danced through the shadows, we twirled in the light,
Turning frowns into laughter, oh what a sight!
The squish of the jelly made us all cheer,
With every breeze, we shed a new tear.

When we finally docked, our hearts were so bright,
It didn't matter, we'd sailed through the night.
With candy and laughter, we ruled the tides,
In this funny voyage, our joy always rides!

Open Seas and Open Hearts

The ocean's a canvas, splashed with delight,
As I painted my dreams on seas, oh so bright!
Pulling my brush through a wave of the blue,
Each stroke was a laugh, each color was new.

A shark done waltzing with a colorful skate,
I paused to giggle at this curious fate.
With jellyfish dancers, we twitched on the floor,
Who knew the sea held such humor galore?

I found a message in a bottle so plain,
It read, 'Stop stressing, go dance in the rain!'
So I danced on the deck, with a seaweed hat,
And twirled and I spun, just like a splashy brat.

So here's to the laughter, the joy it imparts,
With each wave I ride, I'll open my heart.
For life's just a journey, a whimsical spree,
With open seas, we are wild and carefree!

Celestial Navigation of the Soul

Up above, the stars pretend,
To guide my boat, but what a trend!
When I set sail, I always steer,
Right into the drink with no sense of fear.

The compass spins and makes me giddy,
I just hope it won't be too gritty.
Navigating clouds and random signs,
Laughing at Pluto while sipping on brines.

A seagull squawks, is it a clue?
Or just a plain old bird with a view?
I'll trust my gut, not charts or maps,
Especially when I hear those "oops" and "flaps!"

Stars dance around and fish they tease,
Who needs a guide when you've got cheese?
My path may twist, but that's okay,
Through cosmic laughter, I'll find my way.

The Glistening Path of Starlight

Here we skip on glistening dew,
While tripping on shoes that are two sizes too few!
The path ahead sparkles like ice,
But here, my feet think it's rather nice.

With each slip, I laugh and shout,
Who knew I could dance? Watch me flout!
The twinkling lights tease my clumsy feet,
As I glide and giggle to this silly beat.

Fishes giggle as I pass by,
I can't tell if they're winking or just shy.
With every wobble, I bow and grin,
As the universe laughs at my unsteady spin.

The starlit path, full of jests,
Promising journeys and unexpected quests.
Though I trip, I'll always glide,
For laughter's the treasure within this ride.

Hues of a Tumultuous Sky

The sky's a canvas, colors swirl,
A painter's joke in a dizzy whirl.
One minute turquoise, next a beige,
Oh look, there's a rainbow in a rage!

Clouds are huffy, tossing about,
"Who stole my color?" they're sure to shout.
I stand below, wearing a frown,
The sun sticks out its tongue, "Don't drown!"

Lightning cracks jokes, thunder's the punch,
As birds flee faster for lunch.
The hues may clash, but I don't mind,
It's a show that's one of a kind!

With each hue shift, I dodge and weave,
In this wild display, I just believe.
Nature chuckles, oh what a sight,
As I twirl and dance in pure delight.

The Breath of the Seafoam

Bubbles pop and froth take flight,
As waves crash down in pure delight.
The sea sneezes, what a scene,
A salty mist, oh so keen!

It tickles my nose with playful cheer,
"Catch me now, if you dare, my dear!"
I plunge in deep, fists raised high,
Competing with waves, I think I can fly!

Every splash holds a secret to share,
Even crabs chuckle without a care.
They pinch my shorts; oh, what a thrill,
But it's all in good fun, I can't get my fill.

The foam giggles as I tumble and roll,
Where sea creatures watch with a prankster's goal.
With every wave, I know all's well,
For in this laughter, I hear the ocean's spell.

Secrets Carried by Gales

A seagull squawked, then lost its shoe,
It flapped around like it had no clue.
The breeze just laughed, with a playful swirl,
As seabirds danced and the ocean twirled.

A crab in a tux, on a sandy stage,
Took a bow to the wind, in comical rage.
The tide rolled in, with a mischievous grin,
While fish below shared a chuckle or sin.

Seashells giggled, in pastel hues,
Whispering tales of their oceanic views.
A dolphin rolled, with a snicker and flip,
As the current joined in, like a slippery trip.

The wind revealed secrets, as it tousled my hair,
Of mermaids snickering under their lair.
With every gust, laughter did swell,
Carriers of gales, with stories to tell.

Serene Shores and Rolling Waves

At dawn the sun rises, a ball of bright cheer,
While crabs in a conga line give a loud cheer.
Seashells stack up, like towers of play,
While lazy waves whisper, "Let's dance today!"

A starfish sits, with an arm in the air,
Declaring it's winning the 'cool' contest fair.
The tide rolls by, with a wink and a sigh,
As fish in disguise peek up from the fry.

Flips of a dolphin, a somersault show,
While barnacles giggle and give a soft low.
The waves are a blanket, a playful embrace,
As laughter erupts from this watery place.

With a splash and a dash, the breeze swells the fun,
Each moment a treasure, as bright as the sun.
On shores serene, the joy does abide,
With rolling waves playing, a whimsical ride.

Secrets Beneath the Surface

Down in the depths, where the goofballs thrive,
A fish in a bowtie said, "Oh, I'm alive!"
It tickled a turtle with a wink of the eye,
While jellyfish giggled, floating by.

An octopus juggled, with arms all around,
Kicking up bubbles, making soft sounds.
A hidden clam pondered, "What's so funny here?"
While seahorses danced, full of whimsy and cheer.

The coral reef chuckled, in colors so bright,
As a blowfish puffed up in sheer delight.
Laughter erupted from a sea cucumber,
Shaking its body, a bright and goofy bummer.

And as the tide whispered its secrets so sly,
The laughter below made the barnacles cry.
So deep in the ocean, where silliness reigns,
Are treasures of humor that light up the plains.

Where the Water Breathes

Where the surface shimmers, the fun starts to churn,
A catfish in glasses, saying, "Look and learn!"
A whale with a hat, slow dancing with glee,
While squids play jazz in a coral jubilee.

The waves break in laughter, with playful intent,
As bubbles rise up, in a frothy ascent.
Crabs cook up pranks, like culinary art,
Sharing some giggles that tickle the heart.

Beneath the deep blue, where the secrets unwind,
A riddle from flounders, the quirkiest kind.
With every tickle of the sea's gentle breath,
Comes forth the humor, in life and in death.

Amidst the splashes, joy's always a creeper,
Awakening laughter — the ocean's dear keeper.
So splash and be merry, let the fun take its course,
For where the water breathes, humor flows forth!

The Soliloquy of Rolling Surf

The waves are laughing, can't you see?
They joke about sailing, wild and free.
"Catch a fish, or maybe your hat!"
"Watch out, here comes a jumpy brat!"

The gulls are squawking with delight,
"Who's stealing my fries? It's quite a sight!"
Join the dance of splashes and foam,
As sea breezes sing their playful poem.

Sandcastles crumble, they giggle in glee,
Sandworms wiggle, "don't happen to me!"
Laughter erupts from toddlers and mom,
As the sun sets, we all sing a psalm.

Oops! Here comes a wave, so slick,
Splashing the sunscreen; it's quite a trick!
Cheerful chaos in the surf and sun,
Let's laugh at the beach, darling, we've won!

Secrets of Forgotten Shelters

The beach hut whispers tales of old,
'Come gather round, let's share the gold!'
A treasure map drawn in sticky sand,
With a crab as the captain – oh, how grand!

Pelican pals perch with flair,
Stealing snacks from a beachgoer there.
"Got your sandwich? We've got the tooth!"
"Now that's a bite! Come, witness the truth!"

Old flip-flops lying, once worn with pride,
Wish they could join on this wild ride.
"Where's our party? We miss the fun!"
Sunk in the sand, under the sun.

Seagulls are scheming, feathers a-fluff,
Plotting a heist, but is it enough?
Squeezing in laughter, under the shade,
Those secrets wait, till the youths invade!

Harmony in the Coastal Whirl

The tide comes in with a curtsy and swirl,
Dancing shells and seaweed unfurl.
A sand crab claps, so fancy and bright,
Finding a partner in the moonlight!

Clams are a-chatter, gossiping slow,
"Did you hear, that turtle can glow?"
Flip-flops stutter, caught in the dance,
While children giggle, taking a chance.

Octopuses juggle, keeping the beat,
As starfish cheer from their sandy seat.
"Watch this backflip!" the dolphin croons,
Under the gaze of mischievous moons.

It's a carnival near the foamy shore,
Where laughter echoes and spirits soar.
In this whirling mess of waves and cheer,
The coastal comedy thrives year after year!

Sun-Kissed Breezes and Sylvan Shores

The sun sneezes low, giving a wink,
As surfboards try not to sink.
The palms are swaying, gossiping trees,
"Did you hear – that wave barely pleased!"

Crabs wear sunglasses, looking so fine,
Swapping tales of the best brine.
"I once caught a snack, bigger than me!"
"Oh really, my friend? Shell-abrate, tee-hee!"

Seashells giggle, their colors abound,
Making jangly music when tossed around.
"A beach party here, from noon till dusk!"
With fun so bright, it's a happy must!

As the palm fronds dance with a teasing breeze,
And sand spirits play with effortless ease,
We toast to the antics of sun and sea,
Embracing the joy, just come and be free!

Fragments of a Sailor's Soul

He sailed with a banjo on his knee,
While fish sang songs in a symphony.
Every wave a dance, oh what a sight,
But his compass pointed left, not right.

With seagulls dressed in pirate hats,
He'd barter for treasures, maybe some gnats.
His rum was ginger ale in disguise,
He'd laugh so hard, he'd nearly capsize.

Finding driftwood with his name carved,
The sea claimed it back, he just starved.
In a bottle, he found his lost sock,
It winked at him — "You've been quite the shock!"

So let the waves tell tales of his cheer,
As he steers with a laugh and a pint of beer.
For every starlit night in the bay,
He finds a new way to play every day.

Dreams Anchored in the Comfort of Silence

A sailor dreamed of marshmallow skies,
With pancakes afloat, much to his surprise.
He anchored his hope to a bubblegum tree,
Sipping on sunshine, as happy as can be.

The fish wore tuxedos, polite and neat,
Dancing on waves, they skipped to the beat.
"Why's the ocean blue?!" asked a dolphin in glee,
"Because the jellybeans fell from a candy spree!"

With a sail made of laughter, he glided so free,
Chasing the wind, like a playful flea.
The sea whispered secrets, but they came out quite silly,
Like mermaids in hats, doing the dilly-dilly.

In dreams he raced turtles, both fast and spry,
While seagulls cheered, from their perch in the sky.
He woke to the sound of his cat's loud meow,
And realized his dreams were adventures somehow.

The Art of Water's Embrace

Bellyflops turned into graceful dives,
As he splashed with crabs, oh how they thrive!
His training unraveled in flip-flop style,
Sinking like lead, but laughing the while.

Octopuses played cards in the deep,
While algae serenaded him to sleep.
But a pelican snatched his peanut butter,
He chased with a giggle, "You feathery nutter!"

Floating on rafts made of cheese and glee,
He rode the waves, just as free as can be.
A sea turtle winked, "Keep that hat from getting wet,"
He replied, "Never mind! It's my finest duet!"

With each splash and laugh, he changed the tide,
In the embrace of water, fun was his guide.
The ocean, his canvas, painted with jest,
A masterpiece of joy; he sailed with zest.

In Search of Lost Reflections

He searched for his mirror in a fishy bazaar,
Where mirrors were drowned and haunted by stars.
"Is this my reflection, or just a napkin?"
He pondered aloud while the mermaids were clappin'.

The waves giggled softly, "Try looking down!"
But was that a jellyfish or a funny old clown?
He scraped the sea floor with a comical grin,
Finding old shoes and a rusty old tin.

"Okay, who's stealing my delightful image?"
The barnacles laughed, "You were on a scrimmage!"
He juggled floating bottles, as crabs played along,
A seagull squawked, "Join us! You can't go wrong!"

In search of reflections, he let out a cheer,
Finding the fun, he held close with dear.
For laughter's the treasure that sparkles like gold,
In the search for yourself, it never gets old.

Ebbing Thoughts on Shifting Sands

On the beach, my thoughts do dance,
Like a crab that's lost its pants.
Waves chuckle back, they're quite a tease,
Swirling my worries with such ease.

Sandcastles tumble in a breeze,
A royal palace, brought to knees.
Seagulls gossip, perched on high,
They plot my downfall in the sky.

Flip-flops chase the tide for fun,
Oh, what a game—who's won, who's done?
I shout at shells, "You think you're wise?"
They just roll back with salty sighs.

Laughing waves play tricks so sly,
With each lap, they say goodbye.
And here I stand, with sandy toes,
Wondering how it all just flows.

The Horizon's Lullaby

The sun dips low, a sleepy thing,
While gulls are left to dance and sing.
They squawk and leap, a feathery show,
As day drifts off, so soft and slow.

The moon arrives with a silly grin,
"What's the rush? Let the night begin!"
Stars poke out, all twinkly-eyed,
I wave to them, a cosmic guide.

With every sway, the water hums,
"Hey you, land lover! Here it comes!"
I splash about with giggles loud,
As crabs nod approving, feeling proud.

Night's orchestra plays, fine and bright,
A soft serenade, a pure delight.
As I drift off, a peaceful sigh,
I dream of waves that never die.

Flickering Lanterns on Midnight Waters

Balloons of light bob on the sea,
Giggling waves play tricks on me.
The night is young, the laughter wild,
As I chase bubbles, a gleeful child.

Lanterns flicker, like fireflies bold,
Each one whispers secrets untold.
"Dive in deeper!" they seem to glow,
I ponder loudly, "Is that a no?"

A fish jumps high, trying for a dance,
Splashing me with a watery chance.
"Careful now, don't let it win!
Pulling me under, that's quite the sin!"

So I float here, dreaming away,
With shimmering tales in the bay.
Cackles of night, no need to hide,
The lanterns glow, my trusty guide.

Tides of Memory and Mirage

Sandy shores hold memories tight,
As sea oats sway in sheer delight.
I recall building dreams so grand,
With a handful of shells and a pinch of sand.

Mirages dance, they play tricks on sight,
"You think you see? Oh, what a plight!"
I chase after laughter, oh how it skips,
And trips on the waves, then bursts into quips.

Salty kisses upon my cheek,
From playful tides that dance and sneak.
They whisper tales of joy and mirth,
The kind that fills the heart with worth.

Each wave a chuckle, each tide a grin,
They cradle my spirit, let the fun begin.
With every splash, my soul's set free,
In this wondrous world of salty glee.

Soliloquies of Crashing Waves

The waves come in with a splash,
They gossip loud, like a brash.
Each foam is a tale untold,
Of pirate socks and treasures bold.

They tickle toes, they dance and sway,
Chasing crabs who scuttle away.
With each rise, a new joke flies,
The ocean laughs—oh what a surprise!

Seagulls caw like loud comedians,
Stealing fries from the picnic scenes.
"Hey! That's not yours!" the wave declares,
But seagulls just laugh, without any cares.

So let them rant, these ocean jesters,
In salty jest, they're the best investors.
For laughter rolls with the soothing tide,
As we soak in joy, and the waves' wild ride.

Ephemeral Moments in the Fog

In the fog, everything is shy,
A dolphin sneezed, oh my, oh my!
The lighthouse blinked in a playful way,
"Are we lost, or just on holiday?"

Misty whispers floated all around,
Who knew clouds could be so profound?
They giggle softly, brushing by,
Like playful ghosts saying hi, oh hi!

"Is that a sailor, or a kitchen mop?"
The fog chuckles, never wants to stop.
With every corner, it twists and bends,
Turning strolls into silly trends.

Yet in this haze, a truth unfolds,
That every giggle is worth its gold.
So let's toast to the foggy parade,
For silly moments that never fade.

Beyond the Golden Sun

The sun is setting, what a show!
It paints the sky with a golden glow.
The surfers are laughing, wiping out,
In waves of joy, they twist and shout.

"Look, I'm a fish!" one yells with glee,
Flipping and flopping, oh can't you see?
While the gulls squawk, stealing the scene,
Chasing suns in a race so keen.

As the day dips into a warm embrace,
A crab dances—it sets the pace.
"Join me!" he calls, "It's a perfect night!"
Under stars, let's dance, oh, what a sight!

Past the horizon, adventures await,
With laughter echoing, never too late.
So raise a glass to the sun's bowing run,
For the silly fun that's just begun!

Colors in the Ocean's Eye

Oh, look at that coral, it looks like a hat,
A rainbow explosion, how about that?
The fish are all dressed for the grand ball,
With polka dots and stripes—what a colorful thrall!

"Excuse me, sir, do you have the time?"
A crab in a waistcoat, looking so prime.
"Just at six, but who's counting now?
Let's dance in the seaweed, and take a bow!"

Each wave holds a secret, a bright little tale,
Of jellyfish picnics and tales that sail.
So jump in the water, let's make a splash,
In the colorful dance, we're sure to clash!

As the tide takes us on this whimsical ride,
With laughter and colors, let's not hide.
For in this ocean, each moment's a treat,
So dive into joy—with fins on your feet!

The Passage of Time Beneath the Drift

A turtle wore a sun hat, quite a sight,
He danced with the crabs, their moves light.
Seashells giggled, playing hide and seek,
Time flew away, not caring to peek.

The clock said it's ten, but who knew?
Jellyfish clapped, cheering all that they view.
A lobster waltzed, with two left feet,
While starfish laughed, snacking on treats.

The breeze whispered jokes, a soft, silly sound,
As fish made puns, all around.
The sun turned purple, the sky wore a grin,
Day turned to dusk, let the revelry begin!

In this frolicsome tide, laughter prevails,
With seaweed waving like comedic tales.
For time is a friend in this watery sprawl,
Where fun is the jewel, and joy is the call.

Treasures Held in Aquatic Caves

In the deep, where the eels take a snooze,
A treasure chest locked, it just might amuse.
Pirates once laughed, then fell into brine,
Now crabs keep their secrets—what's truly divine?

An octopus came, dressed up just for fun,
With a party hat, he shone like the sun.
Each arm held a snack, oh what a spread!
Even the seaweed wished it was fed!

The fish joined the dance, with bubbles galore,
A party erupted down under the shore.
Underwater jokes flew higher than floats,
As dolphins chimed in with googly-eyed throats!

In caves rich with laughter, the treasures delight,
With giggles and sparkles that shimmer all night.
What's found in the deep is a sight to behold,
With stories of silliness, all waiting to be told.

The Tapestry of the Rolling Ocean

The waves weave tales on the sandy expanse,
Where seagulls are goblins, all ready to dance.
With each twist and turn, the sea plays its role,
Even the barnacles join in the stroll.

The water's a stage, where the waves do pirouettes,
Seashells snap photos, just placing their pet bets.
Sandcastles chuckle, as they topple with grace,
The tides are the dancers, they spin and embrace!

With crabs playing fiddle, and shrimp in a wig,
They host silly soirées, under the moonlit gig.
The dolphins dive deep, and pop back up bright,
While the stars above wink, lending more light.

A swirling cascade of laughter and cheer,
Where each frothy wave brings good vibes near.
In this vibrant ballet, absurdity thrives,
As the tapestry of currents joyfully dives.

Reflections in the Water's Gaze

The mirror-like surface explodes with a cheer,
As fish make funny faces, they've got no fear.
They strike silly poses, and everyone sees,
The turtles join in with some wobbly knees!

Seagulls squawk jokes as they swoop down for fun,
Their shadows cast laughter under the glowing sun.
The ripples all giggle, tickling the shore,
While oysters flash smiles, what a lively score!

Jumping through reflections, the crabs play a game,
Who can make the weirdest face to earn fame?
Fish in the deep give a thumb's up, they drool,
At the antics of sea folks, so merry and cool!

In the water's embrace, where joy bubbles high,
With splashes of humor, that catch every eye.
Life in the blue is a whimsical maze,
Where laughter bounces back from each secret gaze.

Twilight's Gentle Caress

Underneath the evening glow,
Crabs dance like they're in a show.
Waves giggle as they splash the land,
Seagulls squawk, a wacky band.

Stars peek out, oh what a sight,
As clams compete for a noodle fight.
Laughter rides the breezy air,
While fish discuss the latest fare.

Each tide whispers silly tales,
Of mermaids brewing clam cocktails.
The moon chuckles from up high,
While dolphins leap, and sharks just sigh.

In the dusk, we dance and sway,
With silly hats, we'll laugh away.
Under a sky that turns to night,
The ocean giggles, oh what a sight!

The Language of Distant Shores

Whales hum tunes from the deep blue,
While starfish learn the cha-cha too.
Shells gossip about the latest craze,
And octopuses flaunt their stylish ways.

Breezes carry tales from afar,
As crabs rehearse for the next bazaar.
Sandcastles sporting the silliest hats,
While waves tickle the toes of cats.

Every pebble has a story to tell,
Fiddler crabs ring a dinner bell.
Gulls are jesters, making us laugh,
Chasing shadows, they're quite the gaffe.

From shores unknown, chortles sail,
As dolphins gossip without fail.
In this world where laughter shines,
Every moment has fun designs.

Dreams Drifted on the Air

Flying kites like laughing fish,
In the breeze, a playful wish.
Seashells hold the dreams we share,
While waves recite a foamy prayer.

Jellyfish sketch a dance so grand,
Floating lightly, hand in hand.
Whistles in the coral gleam,
While hermit crabs plot their next scheme.

Pufferfish wear their spiky best,
In the ocean, there's no rest.
Sea turtles twist in comical grace,
As laughter bubbles, a merry chase.

Clouds drift by, like cotton candy,
With gulls above, they feel quite dandy.
The currents swirl, a jovial tide,
In this dreamscape, we can't hide!

The Rhythm of Nature's Heartbeat

Crickets click in a jazzy tune,
While stars twirl like the biggest cartoon.
Lizards bask with comical flair,
Sunlight tickling the summer air.

Trees sway to the rhythm of glee,
Bees hum along, busy as can be.
Watermelons join in with a cheer,
As we dance without a care or fear.

The ocean claps with rolling waves,
Fish performing the latest raves.
While otters giggle in a funny caper,
Nature's laugh is a joyful taper.

With every beat, there's fun to find,
In this world, there's magic intertwined.
We sway along to the natural beat,
Where humor and harmony gracefully meet.

The Allure of the Abyss

There once was a sailor named Lou,
Who thought he could catch a big blue.
He dove with a splash,
And came up with trash,
A boot and a fish-shaped shoe.

His friends had a laugh at the sight,
As he danced in the pale moonlight.
He wiggled and twirled,
With a sock he unfurled,
Proclaiming, "I'm ready to bite!"

With seagulls all squawking and grand,
Lou fashioned a hat from the sand.
He declared with a cheer,
"Let's battle the beard,
Of the monster that eats from my hand!"

But the only beast he could find,
Was a crab that was far less than kind.
It pinched at his toe,
Made him shriek, "What a show!"
Then laughed as it danced, quite unwind.

Shimmers in the Dusk's Glow

A lobster named Larry got bold,
He dreamt of adventures untold.
He donned a pink hat,
And said, "How about that?"
To the beach, he would strut, oh so bold!

He met with a finicky shark,
Who claimed he could sing in the dark.
With a gurgle and flail,
He sang like a snail,
And left all the sea critters stark!

The crabs in the sand rolled their eyes,
At a fish trying hard for the prize.
"Here's a tip!" they all said,
"Please stick to your bed,
Just avoid the high notes and cries!"

But Larry kept flaunting his song,
Thinking surely it couldn't be wrong.
He tripped on a shell,
And that was his bell,
As he laughed, "I still feel I belong!"

Tides of Change and Memory

In the surf where the sandpipers play,
A snail had a wonderful day.
He rode on a wave,
And thought he was brave,
Till his shell spun him round in dismay!

With jellyfish jokes up their sleeves,
His pals all burst out in great heaves.
They laughed 'til they cried,
At their friend, who just sighed,
"Next time I'll stick to the leaves!"

The fish joined in on the fun,
With bellyflops under the sun.
The eels wriggled near,
Squeezing laughter and cheer,
As they played hide-and-seek, just for fun!

But nightfall turned smiles into yawns,
As the tide brought in whimsical dawns.
They gathered together,
In all kinds of weather,
And vowed they'd be back with their prawn!

Navigating Through Tempest's Heart

A captain named Melvin was bold,
He swore his ship's name was pure gold.
But when storms would brew,
His crew would all rue,
As the sails flapped like stories retold.

His compass went 'round like a toy,
As it twisted, it filled him with joy.
"Just go with the flow,
Let the laughter grow,
For chaos is what we enjoy!"

He steered through the waves with a grin,
And laughed as the storm pulled them in.
"Hold on!" he would shout,
As the sea tossed about,
"Let's ride on the tide, and begin!"

When they landed on shores made of foam,
They cheered like they'd found out their home.
With seashells in hand,
They did a conga band,
Vowing never again they would roam!

www.ingramcontent.com/pod-product-compliance
Lightning Source LLC
Chambersburg PA
CBHW072119070526
44585CB00016B/1504